Sunshine

Pupil's Book

Class 3

EARLY START EDITION

Cornelsen

Sunshine **Early Start Edition**

Lehrwerk für den früh beginnenden Englischunterricht

Pupil's Book
Class 3

Erarbeitet von
Birgit Hollbrügge, Bielefeld; Ulrike Kraaz, Werther

unter Mitarbeit von
Ines Völtz, Leipzig

Beratende Mitwirkung
Katja Becker, Braunschweig; Karin Freund, Triebes; Evelin Hartmann-Kleinschmidt, Delbrück; Karin Kania, Berlin; Inge Kronisch, Flensburg; Dagmar Lehmann, Tangermünde; Petra Ilona Sälzer, Kamen; Christel Simon, Spreenhagen; Silke Thiel, Erzhausen; Ines Völtz, Leipzig

Verlagsredaktion
Marie Keenoy (Projektleitung), Anne Forder, Elke Lehmann, Penny Paulus, Stefanie Schindewolf

Illustration
Beehive Illustration, Circencester, England: Neil Chapman, Mike Phillips; Mary Hall, Bath, England

Umschlaggestaltung
Karla Detlefsen, Berlin

Layout
Susanne Meyer

Technische Umsetzung
Susanne Meyer; Jana Faust, Berlin

Quellenangaben
Bildquellen A1PIX (S. 36 Father Christmas); Alamy, Abingdon (S. 8 foxgloves: Andrew Compton; S.13 two dogs: image 100, sheep dogs: guy harrop, sit: Daniel Dempster Photography, heel: Kuttig - People, stay and fetch: Arco Images GmbH, good dog: tbkmedia; S.18 lollipop lady with children: Peter Titmuss, lollipop man: SHOUT lollipop sign: Roger Bamber; S.23 doctor: Corbis RF, school girl: Digital Vision, police officers: ilan travel, baker: JUPITER IMAGES / Cornstock Images, footballers: image 100; S.28 rugby: Martin Beddall, tennis: Photofusion Picture Library, hopscotch: Radius Images; S.33 sugar: Tim Hill; S.37 Easter basket: Peter Titmuss, egg rolling: Neil McAllister); Education Photos (S.28 netball); Getty Images (S.36 Christmas tree: Bec Parsons, beach: Getty Images, Christmas dinner: Bec Parsons); Ingram Publishing, Cheshire (S.33 lemon); Jack Wolfskin GmbH & Co. KGaA (S.21 skirt, pullover, jacket, shirt, dress); www.John Birdsall.co.uk (S.14/15); www.mandslibrary.co.uk (S.21 scarf); Marion Schönenberger, Berlin (S.8, 18, 23, 28, 33 Anweisungen); Shutterstock, New York (S.8 poppies: zeber, sunflowers: Leonid Shcheglov, bluebells: Mathew Collingwood, daisies: rimmer; S.13 puppies: Saniphoto, come here: Mircea BEZERGHEANU; S.18 road: GGS, lollipop: Colour; S.21 hat: Rafa Irusta, shoes: Podfoto; S.23 ballerina: Sean Nel; S.28 football: Amy Myers, cricket: Jaco van Rensburg; S.33 cocoa: Switch, pickles: Donald R. Swartz, olives: saim nadir, peanuts: Marc Dietrich, ice cream: Eric Gevaert, grapefruit: Feud Moth, chocolate: Paul Paladin, brezel: Oliver Hoffmann, strawberry: Richard Griffin)
Liedquelle S.18: What do you like? K.: Mark Fishlock, T.: John Foster © Cornelsen 2007

Weitere Bestandteile des Lehrwerkes *Sunshine Early Start Edition*:

Activity Book mit Audio-CD Kurzfassung	ISBN 978-3-464-34688-4
Activity Book mit Audio-CD Kurzfassung und kompletter Lernsoftware	ISBN 978-3-06-031292-4
Lernsoftware	ISBN 978-3-06-031429-4

www.cornelsen.de

1. Auflage, 1. Druck 2009

Druck: CS-Druck CornelsenStürtz, Berlin

ISBN 978-3-464-34691-4

Inhalt gedruckt auf säurefreiem Papier aus nachhaltiger Forstwirtschaft.

Contents

Hello again		4
Unit 1	Meeting friends	6
Unit 2	Pets in the garden	9
Unit 3	At school	14
Unit 4	The second-hand shop	19
Unit 5	Free-time activities	24
Unit 6	In the park	29
Unit 7	Special days	34
Word list		38

Symbols

CD 1.8 listen to the CD · CD 1 track 8

listen

speak

read

play

That's English!

1 Listen to your teacher. Point to the pictures.

2 Work with a partner. Talk about the pictures.

What's in the pictures?
Make a list.

1

2

3

4

English in the classroom

1 Read the dialogues.

2 Talk to a partner.

1

2

3

Hopscotch

CD 1.8 **1** Listen to the CD.
Point to the pictures.

2 Say the numbers.

3 Play hopscotch.

Dialogue: Favourite colours

1 Read the dialogue.

2 Talk to a partner.

In the street

1 Listen to your teacher. Point to the numbers.

CD 1.9

2 Listen to the CD.
What number is Harry's house?

What's in the picture?
Make a list.

Spotlight: Colours

1 Read the texts.

Poppies
are red.

Sunflowers
are yellow.

Bluebells
are blue.

Daisies
are white.

Foxgloves
are pink.

2 Do the experiment.

You need:

a glass of water

blue ink

a white flower

1 Put ink into the glass of water.

2 Put the white flower into the glass of blue water.
Wait.

3 Is the flower white?
Is the flower blue?

2 Pets in the garden

A phone call on Sunday morning

CD 1.16

1 Listen to the CD. Who's calling Harry?

2 Read the speech bubbles.

Dialogue: A phone call

1 Read the dialogue.

2 Talk to a partner.

In the garden shed

1 Look at the picture. What pets are there in the garden shed? What colour are the pets?

CD 1.19

2 Listen to the CD. What are the children's pets?

Do you know more English animal words?

Draw pictures and write the words.

 Ein Bild beschreiben, einen Hörtext verstehen (S.87) · eine Geschichte verstehen (S.92)

Story: Rabbit's party

1 Read the story.

2 Act it out.

Board game: The garden race

1 Play the game.

 Ein Spiel spielen: Redemittel anwenden (S.95)

Spotlight: Dogs

1 Read the texts.

Golden Retrievers are big.
Jack Russells are small.

Baby dogs are called puppies.

Dogs can learn lots of things.

2 Read the speech bubbles.

3 Talk about the pictures.

1

2

3

4

5

6

A day at school

1 Look at the pictures. Talk about the pictures.

CD 1.27

2 Listen to the CD. Point to the pictures.

3 Read.

Work with a dictionary.

Write a list of school words.

1

This is a school bus.

2

3

The children are playing hopscotch.

Landeskundliche Informationen verstehen, einen Hörtext verstehen, Sätze lesen (S.103)

7

The children are eating lunch at school.

Story: Jack's bad day

CD 1.30

1 Listen to the story.

2 Read the story.

Eine Geschichte verstehen und selber lesen (S.109)

Game: Take five

1 Read the text.

2 Play the game in groups of four.

① Take five cards from each pupil's word box:

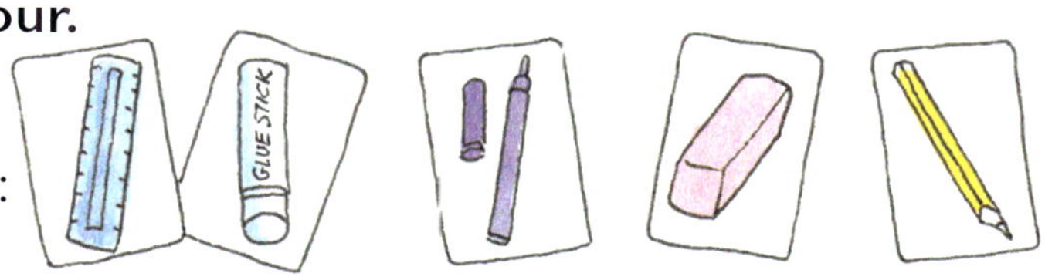

② Put all the cards together.

③ Shuffle the 20 cards.

④ Give five cards to each child.

⑤ Ask the questions.

Spotlight: School in Britain

1 Read the texts.

A lollipop man helps children to cross the street.

Look right.
Look left.
Look right again.
Cross the street, please.

This is a lollipop lady.

A street in Britain.
Why must you look right?

The lollipop sign tells people to stop.

A lollipop – mmm.

2 Make a safety badge.

You need:

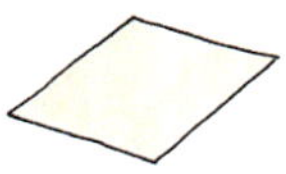
cardboard

black, yellow and red felt tips or coloured pencils

scissors

a safety pin

sticky tape

1 Draw a circle on the cardboard.
Colour the badge.
Write your words.

2 Cut out the badge.

3 Stick a safety pin on the back with sticky tape.

Here's your safety badge.

Texte lesen, Informationen entnehmen, einen Anstecker basteln (S.193)

At the second-hand shop

1 Look at the shop. Talk about the shop.

2 Read the words. Find the pictures.

What's in the shop?

Write a list.

There's …

There are …

pullover

trousers

dress

hat

skirt

shoes

gloves

What is he wearing?

1 Work with a partner. Look at the pictures. What are the children wearing?

Sarah

Harry

Kate

Samir

Emily

John

Wortschatz und Redemittel festigen (S.123)

Dialogue: Clothes

1 Read the dialogue.

2 Talk to a partner.

Story: A funny boy

1 Look at the pictures. Talk about the pictures.

2 Read the story.

Eine Geschichte lesen (S.131)

Spotlight: Clothes

baker · dancer
doctor · football players
police officers · school girl

1 Clothes can tell you about people.
Read the texts and say what these people do.

1

The … is wearing a white coat.

2

The … is wearing school uniform.

3

The … are wearing uniforms.

4

The … is wearing a tutu.

5

The … is wearing a white shirt and a white hat.

6

The … are wearing blue football shirts.

2 Make a book. Play the game.

You need:

a work-sheet

scissors

a stapler

coloured pencils

1 Colour the pictures.

2 Cut out the book.

3 Staple the book together.

Song: What do you like?

1 Look at the pictures. Talk about the pictures.

CD 2.3 **2** Listen to the song. Point to the pictures.

3 Sing the song.

1

2

3

Dialogue: Free-time activities

1 Read the dialogue.

2 Talk to a partner.

Rhyme: Where's the cat?

CD 2.7

1 Listen to the rhyme. Point to the pictures.

2 Read the rhyme.

Where's the cat? Where's the cat?
Is she in the living room – watching TV?
Is she in the kitchen – drinking my tea?

Where's the cat? Where's the cat?
Is she in the bedroom – eating my shoe?
Is she in the bathroom – playing with shampoo?

Where's the cat? Where's the cat?
There she is – sleeping in Mum's favourite hat.

Spot the difference

1 **Look at the pictures. Where's Harry in house number 1? Where's Harry in house number 2?**

2 **Talk to a partner. What furniture is in the house?**

What's in the house?

Work with a dictionary.

1

2

Aussagen zu Bildern treffen: Wortschatz festigen, Möbelwörter wiederholen (S.148)

Story: The babysitters

CD 2.8

1 **Listen to the CD. Point to the right pictures.**

2 **Read the story.**

CD 2.8

3 **Listen again. What picture is in the story?**

Spotlight: Sports and games

1 Read the texts.

Children in Britain like playing sports and games.

1 
football

2 
rugby

3 
cricket

4 
tennis

5 
hopscotch

6 
netball

2 Play the game "Eggety Budge".

You need:
a ball

1 Each child has a number.
2 One child throws the ball and shouts a number.
3 The child with the right number catches the ball.
The other children run.
4 The child with the ball shouts, "Eggety Budge".
5 The child takes three big steps.
6 He hits another child with the ball.

6 In the park

A day in the park

1 Look at the picture. Talk about the picture.

2 Find the numbers. Say: Number 10 is on …

What do you like doing in the park?

Make a list.

Rhyme: I eat apples

CD 2.13

1 Listen to the rhyme.

2 Look at the pictures. Point to the right pictures.

3 Read the rhyme.

I eat apples – crunch, crunch, crunch.
I eat peaches – munch, munch, munch.
I eat oranges – lick, lick, lick.
I eat ice cream – quick, quick, quick.

I eat strawberries – chew, chew, chew.
I eat lemons – eww, eww, eww.
I eat cherries – click, click, click.
I eat ice cream – quick, quick, quick.

Einen Reim lesen (S.159)

At the kiosk

1 **Talk about the picture. How much is an orange juice? How much are the peanuts?**

CD 2.15 **2** **Listen to the CD. Which ice cream does the boy want?**

Dialogue: Buying ice cream

1 **Read the dialogue.**

2 **Talk to a partner**

Story: Where's my ice cream?

CD 2.16

1 Listen to the story.

2 Read the story. Is it right or wrong?

 Einen Hörtext verstehen, eine Geschichte lesen (S.165)

Spotlight: Taste

1 Read the texts.

2 Talk about the pictures.

Your tongue can taste sweet things. Sugar tastes sweet.

Your tongue can taste sour things. Pickles taste sour.

Your tongue can taste bitter things. Cocoa tastes bitter.

Your tongue can taste salty things. Olives taste salty.

3 Do the experiment.

You need:

honey

salt

lemon juice

cocoa

four glasses of water

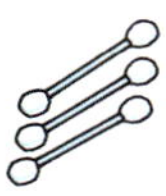
cotton buds

1 Mix the water with honey, salt, lemon juice and cocoa.

2 Dip a cotton bud into a glass.

3 Touch your tongue at the back, on the sides and in the front. Where's the taste?

4 Talk about your taste.

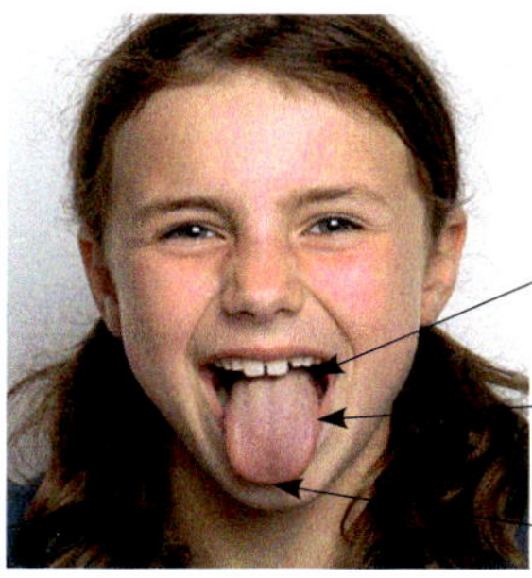

What can you taste …

at the back of your tongue?

on the sides of your tongue?

at the front of your tongue?

7 Special days

Birthdays

CD 2.18

1 Listen to the song.

2 Talk about the picture.

3 Sing the song.

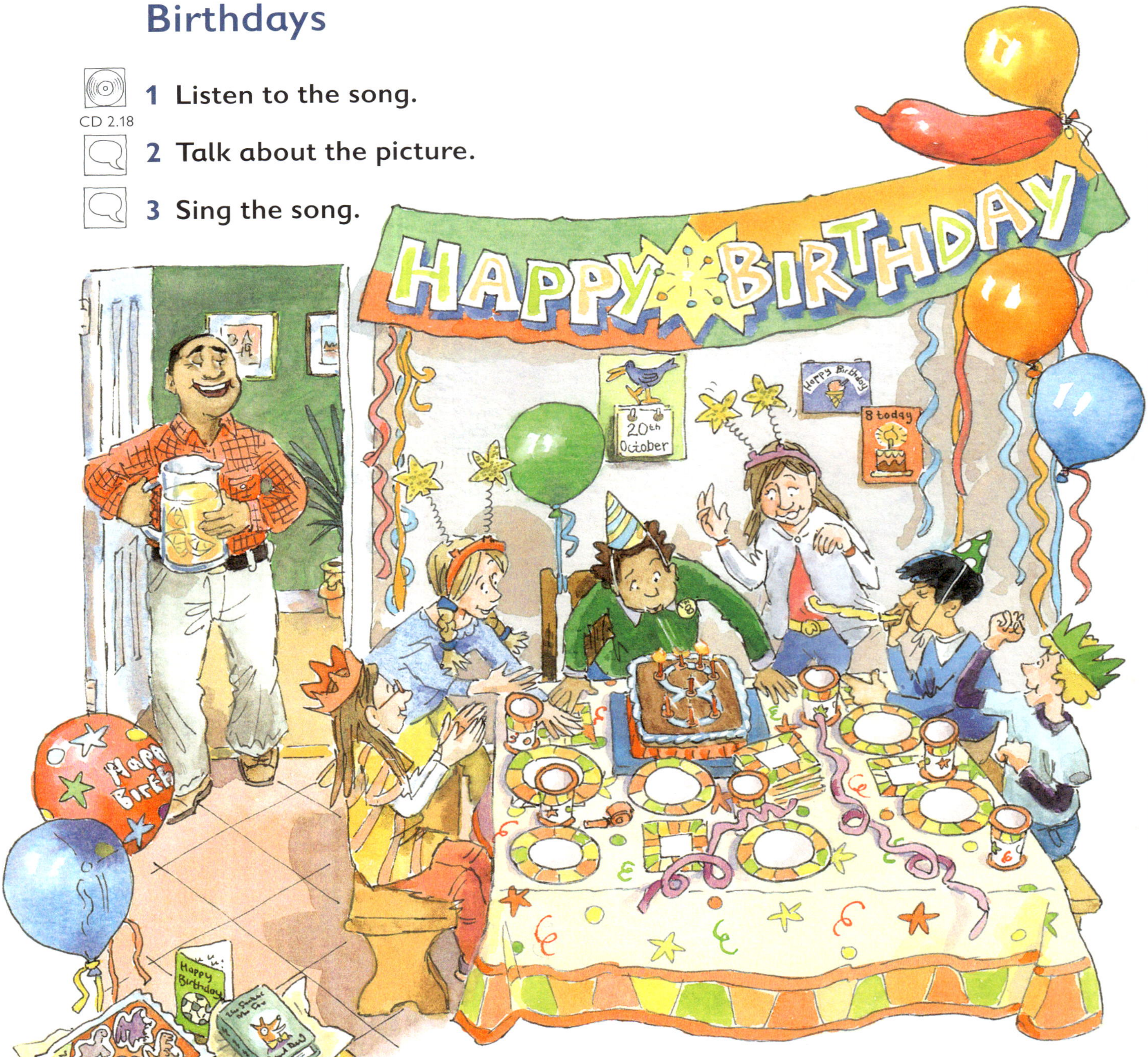

Birthday song

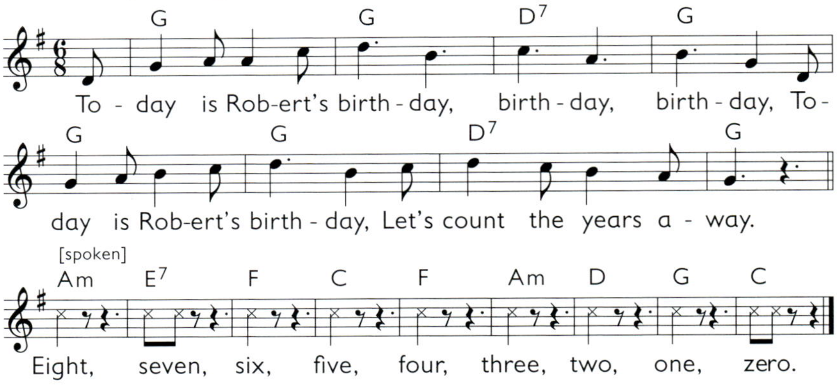

Ein Lied lernen, sich zu einem Bild äußern (S.173)

Halloween

1 Talk about the picture. Count the ghosts, monsters, pumpkins, skeletons, …

2 Listen to the rhymes.
CD 2.21

3 Read the rhymes.

Trick or treat,
Listen to the beat.
We want only
Sweets to eat.

Trick or treat,
Smell my feet.
Give me something
Good to eat!

Christmas in Australia

1 Look at the pictures. Talk about the pictures.

2 Listen and point.

3 Read the texts.

1

2

Here's our Christmas tree.

3

Christmas on the beach

4

This is Father Christmas in Australia.

5

Our family on Christmas Day

Landeskundliche Informationen erfahren, Wortschatz üben (S.181)

Easter

1 Look at the pictures. Talk about the pictures.

2 Read the texts.

3 Sing the song.

CD 2.25

Here's an Easter basket.

Children like playing Easter games.

Chocolate Easter eggs – mmm!

Here's the Easter bunny.

Word list

A

again nochmals
apple Apfel

B

°**badge** Anstecker
°**baker** Bäcker
°**ball** Ball
banana Banane
bath Badewanne
bathroom Badezimmer
bed Bett
bedroom Schlafzimmer
behind hinter
big groß
birthday Geburtstag
birthday cake Geburtstagskuchen
birthday card Geburtstagskarte
birthday present Geburtstagsgeschenk
°**bitter** bitter
°**bluebell** Glockenblume
black schwarz
blue blau
book Buch
boring langweilig
°**Britain** Großbritannien
brown braun

C

can können
°**cardboard** Karton
carrot Möhre
cat Katze
°**catch** fangen
chair Stuhl
cherry Kirsche
chocolate Schokolade
Christmas Weihnachten
Christmas Day Weihnachtstag (25.12.)
Christmas Eve Heiligabend (24.12.)
Christmas tree Weihnachtsbaum
coat Mantel
°**cocoa** Kakao
colour 1. Farbe 2. ausmalen
°**coloured pencils** Buntstifte
come kommen
°**cotton bud** Wattestäbchen
°**cricket** Kricket
°**cross the street** die Straße überqueren
°**cut out** ausschneiden

D

°**daisy** Gänseblümchen
°**dancer** Tänzer/-in
°**dip** tunken
°**doctor** Arzt/Ärtzin
dog Hund
draw zeichnen
dress Kleid
drink 1. Getränk 2. trinken

E

Easter Ostern
Easter basket Osterkorb
Easter bunny Osterhase
Easter egg Osterei
eat essen
eight acht
eighty achtzig
eleven elf

F

Father Christmas Weihnachtsmann
favourite Lieblings-
feet Füße
felt tip Filzstift
°**Fetch.** Bring!
fifty fünfzig
five fünf
°**flower** Blume
food Essen
football Fußball

°**football player** Fußballspieler/-in
forty vierzig
four vier
°**foxglove** Fingerhut
funny lustig

G

garden shed Gartenhaus
ghost Gespenst
°**glass** Glas
gloves Handschuhe
glue stick Klebstift
green grün
guinea pig Meerschweinchen

H

hamster Hamster
hat Mütze
°**Heel.** Bei Fuß!
help helfen
here hier
°**hit** schlagen
°**honey** Honig
hopscotch Himmel und Hölle
house Haus

I

ice cream Eiscreme
in in
°**ink** Tinte
in-line skates Inlineskates

J

jacket Jacke
juice Saft

K

kitchen Küche

L

lamp Lampe
°**learn** lernen
°**left** links
lemon Zitrone
lettuce Salat
like mögen
listening to music Musik hören
living room Wohnzimmer
°**lollipop** Lutscher
°**lollipop man/lollipop lady** Schülerlotse/Schülerlotsin
lunch Mittagessen
lunch box Brotdose

M

meeting friends Freunde treffen
milk Milch
°**mix** mischen
monster Monster
mountain bike Mountainbike

N

°**netball** Korbball
nine neun
ninety neunzig
number Zahl

O

°**olive** Olive
on auf
one eins
open öffnen
orange 1.Apfelsine 2.orange
orange juice Orangensaft
oven Backofen

P

peach Pfirsich
peanut Erdnuss
pen Füller
pencil Bleistift
pencil case Federmappe
pencil sharpener Bleistiftspitzer
pet Haustier
°**pickle** Essiggurke
pink rosa
play spielen
playing computer games Computerspiele spielen
playing football Fußball spielen

please bitte
°**police officer** Polizist/-in
°**poppy** Mohnblume
pullover Pullover
°**puppy** Welpe
pumpkin Kürbis

R

rabbit Kaninchen
rat Ratte
read lesen
red rot
reindeer Rentier
°**right** rechts
rubber Radiergummi
°**rugby** Rugby
ruler Lineal
°**run** rennen

S

°**safety pin** Sicherheitsnadel
°**salt** Salz
°**salty** salzig
scarf Schal
school Schule
school bag Schultasche
school bus Schulbus
°**school girl** Schülerin
scissors Schere
seven sieben
seventy siebzig
shirt Hemd
shoes Schuhe
°**shout** rufen
°**Sit.** Sitz!
six sechs
sixty sechzig
skateboard Skateboard
skeleton Skelett
skirt Rock
small klein
sofa Sofa
°**sour** sauer
spider Spinne
°**staple** zusammenheften
°**stapler** Tacker
°**Stay.** Bleib!
°**step** Schritt
°**sticky tape** Klebstreifen
stocking Strumpf
strawberry Erdbeere
°**street** Straße
°**sugar** Zucker
°**sunflower** Sonnenblume
°**sweet** süß

T

table Tisch
°**talk about** über etwas reden
°**taste**
1. Geschmackssinn 2. schmecken
ten zehn
°**tennis** Tennis
thirty dreißig
three drei
°**throw** werfen
toilet Toilette
°**tongue** Zunge
°**touch** berühren
°**train** trainieren
trousers Hose
°**tutu** Tutu (Ballettrock)
twelve zwölf
twenty zwanzig
two zwei

U

under unter
understand verstehen
°**uniform** Uniform

W

watching TV fernsehen
°**water** Wasser
wardrobe Kleiderschrank
white weiß
witch Hexe

Y

yellow gelb

°Wörter von den *Spotlight*-Seiten.